A BOOK ABOUT NOBODY

Can Crazy be **Normal**?

DAVID M FINE

REGISTERED PSYCHOTHERAPIST (RET.) AND CERTIFIED LIFE COACH

CONTENTS

INTRODUCTION

CAN A BOOK about "nobody" be as interesting as a book about "somebody"? You know the "somebodies" I am talking about. Those movie stars, political figures, sports heroes and rock legends who, if they were to publish a book, would have people flocking to buy it. What about the "nobodies" of the world? Would people flock to a book written by "nobodies"? Could their lives be as interesting as a "somebody"? Could they be embroiled in as much drama? Why don't we find out? Maybe you will learn a thing or three along the way.

I am a retired Registered Psychotherapist and presently certified as a Life Coach. "Meh, not a big deal", you're probably thinking. But actually, I *did* face incredible odds and made it past Grade 8 (contrary to predictions at the time). Doesn't seem like much, but for a fearful guy like me back then, it was quite a feat.

Through this book, I will share my private stories with you. I will welcome you fully into my life. I'll share some (embarrassing) thoughts and moments that many people would choose to hide in the effort to look "normal". I've always thought that appearing to be normal isn't all it's cracked up to be. I believe that many of us, in our efforts to appear normal, have been left with self-esteem issues, an anxious way of being and paranoia. There are some situations in this book that many in society would be shocked at disclosing. We hide thoughts about ourselves because we don't think we will be accepted by society. In my mind, I think this is where we're flawed as humans. Nowadays, we have access to a host of avenues for support – why not reach out and disclose in a safe space and in an appropriate manner? I think you'll be pleasantly surprised at how many people have gone through the same experiences and share the same challenges.

The definition of normal is "Conforming to a standard, usual, typical or expected". How boring. Who needs that! What is the worst that can happen if we don't act "normal"? People may judge us or possibly worse, we judge ourselves. It's not death, but you could be shunned by many. You might even lose your job by not conforming. No wonder so many people dislike their work. Conforming to someone else's idea of normal sucks. Nothing against a boss, it is just the way it has all been laid out.

Things that were considered *abnormal* behaviour thirty years ago are now being accepted. So, if it is being accepted in the present, does that mean it is now normal… or was it always normal and it just scared the hell out of some of us?

The point is, being human is a normal thing and therefore all thoughts in a human's mind are normal. Does it mean it is *right*? Not necessarily, but it is *human*.

My first book, *Understanding Clarity*, was more a reference guide to life's dilemmas and how to work through issues in a logical fashion. This took a lot of work and concentration on my part and the years of experience in my field of Psychotherapy enabled me to create this guide. This second book, *A Book about Nobody*, is more about my upbringing and experiences through my stages of life. These challenges gave me some of my insights that enabled me to create the guide in my first book.

In reading this book, some of you might be able to find familiarity with the growth stages in your own lives.

So here we go... the good, the bad and the ugly. Some will love me, some will see me as courageous, others might detest me and some will just write me off as an older man who is losing his marbles. After reading this book, others might have trouble carrying on a conversation with me without thinking of a number of the topics I shared. I suggest you look at "some of the things" you hold private and would never disclose, and try not to judge me too harshly. You may even find the strength to examine your own private thoughts more closely.

You will see my issues and I had lots. You will see my illogical thinking and how I grew more conscious of my craziness. Oh well, as my Dad used to say, "You are a long time dead". A hundred years from now who is going to care about this book or anything else? Hopefully by watching me wrestle with my stuff, you'll also gain some insights into how to work through your irrational, but normal human thinking.

I will use very few names throughout this book as most people wanted to remain anonymous.

ONE

MOMENTS IN MY CHILDHOOD NEVER WANT TO GO THROUGH THAT AGAIN!

I WAS CONCEIVED IN Orillia, Ontario, a beautiful little resort town on Lake Couchiching. I was born into a middle-class conservative Jewish family. On the surface of it, we were just another suburban family—but the truth of it was much more complicated. My Dad was an entrepreneur and owned a jewelry store. He seemed to do quite well at it, but you wouldn't know from talking to him. (We'll get to that later.) He was a fairly good-looking man who took pride in his appearance and was in good physical shape.

My Mom started off as a teacher, but she didn't continue

in her career for long. Mom only had one year of university so she taught the first grades at a school on Niagra on the lake where the younger grades were combined. She only lasted one year and she told my sister she quit when she discovered the Superintendent of schools was coming to observe her.

She ended up helping Dad in his business, probably to save on labour costs and she was too insecure to do anything else. She hired a nanny to take care of my siblings and me.

My eldest brother was five years older than me, and my sister a year and a half older. When my older brother was born my mother referred to him as a "Mongoloid". Where my Mom came up with these thoughts, I never understood. "Mongoloid" is an offensive and dated term that was often used to refer to indigenous people in Asia. Today some people use it to refer to people who have Down Syndrome. Understandably I don't like the word as she referenced to it. When we were older, Mom used to joke about his looks when he was a child, and comment that, "only a mother could love his face". I thought that he looked a bit different than the rest of us when he was a child, but Mom was embarrassed in some way. Maybe she thought that he looked more like a Neanderthal Caveman with primitive features. He ended up being a good-looking guy.

I found my older brother to be very quiet and sensed that he was angry most of the time. I could have been mistaken but to me, he just felt uncomfortable in our family. I'm not sure what that was all about. I used to have a million questions for my big brother. I thought he didn't have the patience for me. Part of me couldn't blame him as I talked a good deal of gibberish and was so curious. I worshipped him for quite a long time. Perhaps because I didn't feel I had a father who wanted to spend time with me. My older brother seemed just so cool. We ended up not being very close, (but there was a time later in my life when I reached out to him and he seemed to be so much more compassionate).

My older sister… well, I wasn't very close to her while growing up. She did tell me she used to beat me up regularly until I grew older and could beat her up. I remember when I was in high school, guys used to come up to me and talk about my sister's legs. Mini skirts were all the rage back then. I always thought she was an attractive woman. I recall my sister being there for me during my struggles with my first marriage.

Back to me. I had to be one of the cutest little babies ever born. Wavy, curly brown hair, a little pudgy with a dimple in my chin and just all around gorgeous. My mother was so proud. Everyone liked me. As I started to grow up, my personality was one of innocence and cooperation, but I was full of questions and so badly wanted to communicate with others. I was given loads of attention. Maybe my looks and mannerisms were a curse, as the attention and love didn't last.

The turning point came when my baby brother was born and I was five years old. It seemed as if my mother started having problems then. It was also a turning point for me. My baby brother was pudgy and cute—not as cute as me, but that didn't matter. As far as I was concerned, this would be the beginning of the end.

I remember the day my mother came home from the hospital with him. As usual, I had a million questions for her. She screamed at me. Her face was filled with disgust—something I had never witnessed before. She told me to leave her alone. I was shocked beyond belief. The whole family was cowering from her craziness.

From that day on, I knew I was no longer the "special one". I was no longer number one. My younger brother had taken this spot. After five years of being showered with attention (and what I perceived as love), I was now catapulted to being a "nobody".

Thinking back, I believe this is when my low self-esteem issues began. It sometimes crosses my mind that I could have been confident and grown up to be quite successful if only my younger brother hadn't been born. But the opposite had taken place. At the tender age of five, I lost all my self- esteem and confidence. I would continue to nosedive as you will discover.

My intention to get attention and be number one again didn't stop right away. I used to have a habit of running into my parents' bedroom first thing in the morning complaining of a belly-ache. I didn't want to go to school. I was in Grade 1 and school frightened me to death. Sometimes they would let me stay home, sometimes they wouldn't. Home was the only safe place. Well, compared to school it seemed that way. I was caught between a rock and a hard place.

They took me to a psychiatrist who had this metal circular instrument on his forehead and wore a white lab coat. He looked like a cyclops or a crazy scientist. I imagined that the metal circular instrument could see inside my brain. He was of little help, but he noticed that I wanted my Mom's attention most of the time. He had told my parents that I wouldn't make it past Grade 8. I would be a "special needs kid" or whatever they called it back then. Meanwhile, I kept on complaining about a sore stomach and it finally got to the point where my mother didn't know what to do. She sat me down at one point and said, "if you don't stop this I will have your appendix cut out". I didn't quite understand the relationship between my complaining and appendix at that age, but I continued to run into their bedroom pleading to stay home.

One day she came up to me and said, "that's it, you are having it cut out and then you will have no reason to complain". Before I knew it, I was in a hospital and it seemed like a dozen doctors with masks were sticking me with a multitude of needles in order to put me to sleep. They took out my appendix and it was negative. There was nothing wrong.

It was not the solution to my fears, but it accomplished two things: I never ran into my parent's bedroom complaining about a stomach-ache again; I also believe it caused an impotence issue. It seemed I started to believe that if I complained in life, my mother would cut "it" out. And I suppose you can imagine what "it" is. This issue will pop up (excuse the pun) as my story continues.

I almost failed Grade 1, but for some reason they

allowed me to pass. I wasn't a slow kid, just scared to death of the world. My Mom didn't understand me at all.

In Grade 2, my attention issues crept up again. I told the girl sitting in front of me that I was blind. She freaked out and yelled, "David is BLIND" to the rest of the class. The teacher ignored me and laughed. I think she knew a little bit about my dramatics. I had a major crush on this teacher. She was big-framed, tall, good looking, and the best part of all was that she wore tight-fitting tops. She was buxom, like an Amazon. The girl in front of me started yelling, "It isn't fair that you're ignoring him. He is literally blind." The teacher finally got up and carried me down to the nurse. Being cuddled by this voluptuous woman, was the highlight of my day (or year). The blindness ploy had gotten me what I wanted. At the nurse's office, I finally came out of my supposed blindness and said, "I don't know what happened but I'm better." I figured I could only go so far with this fake malady.

In the same class, another boy seemed to want attention but he didn't have a similar outcome. He was a trouble-maker, joking and carrying on. The teacher couldn't settle him down, so consequently, she sent him down to the principal. I don't know if it was on purpose or not, to warn students to behave better, but the loudspeaker (or P.A. system as it was called back then) was on. The student started screaming uncontrollably. The principal was hitting him on the hand with a strap. It must have gone on for what seemed like ten minutes. The whole school heard it. Try that today in the year 2019!

A few embarrassing moments from my childhood that have stayed with me...

I recall an incident when the town bully spat in my face as I was on my way home from school. Being the scared kid I was, I ignored him. I still think about that incident to this day. I saw myself as a coward. This type of behaviour was to show itself again later in my life.

On my way to school one day, someone walking behind me said, "how come you're always *marching* to school?" At the time I didn't understand what he meant and thought he was just making fun of me. Actually, he was quite observant and my "marching" was an indication that something was indeed wrong with me physically. It was something that later caused issues for more than just me. But we'll get there later.

I remember once when we were in Hebrew School, my older brother and his friend had just stolen some cutlery from the restaurant where they had dined. They told me to return it or they might go to jail. I took it back for them and the owner thanked me. When I went back to Hebrew School, my brother and his friend were rolling over laughing and they said, "We wouldn't have gone to jail. The manager must have thought you were nuts." I thought I was a fool.

At this point, I want to mention some childhood experiences with my mother that directly affected both me and my siblings.

In all the time I knew my mother, I only remember one time I found her loving and in a good mood. I was outside on a beautiful spring day sitting on the front lawn waiting for the bread man to deliver the baked goods. Mom came out with a big smile on her face and told me I could pick out anything I wanted. I picked out jelly donuts. She seemed in such a good mood and I loved her at that moment. What a safe relaxed feeling it was, even though it was fleeting.

She had told me once, "David, if you find happiness *one* day a year you are doing well." I wondered if this was true. I decided it was something that wasn't worth giving serious thought to. Even at that young age, I refused to believe that.

I once heard my mother chasing my older brother all over the house. My brother was in a panic and doing his best to apologize. He sat down at the piano and she was screaming at the top of her lungs. She was whipping him and telling him to obey her or else! My brother was crying, tears rolling down his face and I told her to stop. I was frightened of her, but my brother was so upset and I felt so sorry for him. She wouldn't stop screaming and whipping him. She'd lost it, all because he hadn't practiced the piano that day.

About a week later, I was playing across the street at one of my friend's houses. Their house had no grass yet and the front yard was completely full of mud as it had just finished raining. My Mom had bought me new shoes. At some point, I came home and left my shoes by the door, not even thinking I had done anything wrong. I was probably in Grade 2 or 3. Before I knew it, my mother was screaming like a banshee. She said, "David come here." It was one of the most frightening things I had ever heard. When I sheepishly went to her, she had her fists up like a boxer and started punching me uncontrollably. I fell to the ground and she started kicking me relentlessly with the toe of her shoe. When I begged her to stop, she said, "Well if you didn't fall to the ground I wouldn't be kicking you." But she would have been hitting me with her fists. Finally, she grew tired and walked away. I hated her in that moment. All because of a pair of muddy shoes.

There was a time when I was about 8 years old when I had the flu. I didn't make it to the toilet one night and had vomited in the hallway. My mother came out and wouldn't stop screaming at me. I can understand the irritation of having one of your children throw up in the hallway in the middle of the night, but in my condition and at such a young age, a little bit of sympathy would have gone a long way.

I once confided in my mom about a rather embarrassing story about myself. I can't for the life of me remember what it was about, but I made her promise under no circumstances to tell anyone. She promised. About a week later, my cousins who lived a few houses down the street were laughing at me and I wondered why.

At that point, I realized that the person I should have been able to trust the most, who I should have been able to confide in the most, who should have nurtured me the most, had revealed my secret.

I never told my mother a thing in confidence again. It taught me that if I couldn't trust my mother, then I couldn't trust anybody.

⁓

At one stage I started taking singing and piano lessons. I was not skilled at playing the piano. All my siblings were much more talented, and at the time I wondered why I didn't have the talents they had. As it turns out this was related to the comment about me "marching" to school (but more about this later). Unfortunately, as I continued to develop, it became obvious that my siblings were considerably more talented than I was in most activities. My Mom self- diagnosed me—she told all our relatives and friends that I was "retarded". People told me what she had said and they were quite upset about it. "Retarded" is such a negative and offensive term for mentally handicapped. Was I really mentally handicapped? I didn't think I was, but shouldn't a mother know her own child? To back up her diagnosis, she said that the doctors had held me in the womb for too long and therefore I didn't get enough air to the brain. I believed that story for many years. At some point, I was told how silly that thinking was. I would have continued to receive air and the nutrients I required even if my birth was delayed.

My mother never laid a hand on my sister, contrary to how she dealt with my brother and I. I never saw her get upset with her, but my sister had stories to tell. I remember her once telling me about an incident when they were at the Opera House in Orillia. Mom made some derogatory comment about a woman who was in a wheelchair. The woman in the wheelchair was causing a sort of traffic jam in the aisle and it was difficult for other people to leave at the end of the concert. Mom said, "stupid crippled people should stay at home. They just get in everybody's way."

That would come back to haunt her in the future. My sister was quite upset at our Mom for the insensitive comments.

My sister wasn't a fan of our mother as she explained to me later in life. I'm not sure exactly how she offended my sister, but she did mention that our mother would be very direct with her opinions. To my way of thinking, the problem with my Mom's approach was that she would get very upset when someone was direct with her or had a difference of opinion. Mom was always right. You did not disagree with her.

I must admit that my younger brother also received no abuse from our mother. I believe that she lost her motivation to hurt us as she got older. But he didn't get a free ticket. My younger brother was pudgy when he was growing up. Dad used to call him "fatty" and "porky" a lot of the time. Understandably, this irritated my brother to no extent. I think I sort of liked it. I always thought he had been spoiled because, to me, it seemed that he never got into crap like my older brother and I, as mentioned above. As I alluded before, Dad was physically fit and exercised all the time. I believe he was embarrassed at having an overweight kid. That said, this was much more about Dad's insecurities than anything else. In some way, although Dad's words were cruel, they did seem to be effective, though I'm sure they left their scars. My younger brother lost his weight after high school. Even into his sixties, he stays thin and healthy like all of us siblings.

On a side note, I want to mention that this also had an effect on me. To this day I am very conscious of my weight. It is a blessing and a curse. The blessing is, it keeps me healthy and regulates my IBS. The curse is, it haunts me daily managing my food intake and exercising seven days a week. I feel like a prisoner of my own making not allowing myself to slip for one minute. I understand the source of this but I chose to continue for the time being. We do have the right to make choices in our life. Not all of our thinking has to be rectified at the moment we see a problem. Just be aware it is there.

Back to my brother.

Mom told my younger brother when he was a baby that she wanted to drop him on his head and end his life, as he wasn't a girl. Well, you can't say she didn't tell her truth! We had such supportive parents…

And yet, later on in life when Mom was living in her own apartment, my younger brother took care of her for years. He would run her errands and see to all the other miscellaneous issues. I know it was quite a depressing atmosphere for him. He felt he was stuck.

Enough about my mom, well at least for the moment. My one claim to fame was my singing but I didn't fare well at the Kiwanis festivals (regional music festivals held across Canada). I came last in my group and it bothered me immensely as it was more proof of how pathetic I was. I decided to practice incessantly for the next year's competition. I won all firsts and received a $25.00 scholarship. This was, of course, a lot more money back then, than it is today.

I was obligated to perform in front of hundreds of people at the opera theatre in order to receive this scholarship and I had never felt so dreadful in my life. I decided after that performance to quit. I said singing in a soprano voice was not manly at twelve years old. The truth was that my confidence was lacking and I was so frightened to continue. I have often regretted this decision. It was the one thing I excelled at, but without the confidence, it didn't matter how talented I was. This holds true for most of us.

I always thought that being "famous" was the ultimate key to success. The proof was obvious. To get people to worship me, I would have to be successful. Many Hollywood stars are treated like gods and goddesses. Everyone wants to get close to them. My mistaken belief was that this would boost my self-esteem. But I can promise you my self-esteem would still have been lacking, even if I were famous.

You can't correct low self-esteem from the outside.
It has to be done from the inside.

Then came my Bar Mitzvah, the hugely celebrated occasion to mark when a Jewish boy becomes a man at the age of 13.

My parents were not very religious. The family was considered "Conservative". "Orthodox" were the most religious and observed all the rituals of the Jewish Religion. From my perspective, "Reformed" was a newer religion, which relaxed the rules to some extent. As Conservatives, we observed the "High Holidays", and went to Hebrew School, but the weekly traditions were not observed. My Dad took religion much more seriously in his later years. My siblings and I really didn't seem to take it all too seriously and a couple of us observed the "High Holidays", but that was it. I observed the "High Holidays" so my kids would be introduced to the religion.

For me, the Bar Mitzvah felt like the biggest farce. I was no *man*. At the morning service, the Rabbi spoke about how I would attend synagogue every Saturday and would perform the tefillin ritual every morning. This would never happen. Religion was not for me. I saw God as a punisher with little capability for forgiveness. I felt quite shameful.

Even though I felt like this deep down, I blew the congregation away when I sang all the prayers in the morning Bar Mitzvah service. I was confident (probably because people wouldn't expect a Bar Mitzvah boy to have such a good voice). No expectation. Then there was the sprawling luncheon put on by my parents in my honour. My parents had given me a choice the year before: either have a huge luncheon for the extended family, or my Dad would use the money to give me a piece of land to invest in. I know Dad was very disappointed when I picked a party. I was 12 years old at the time… what did I know about investments? My Dad saw the party as a waste of money.

As I grew older, I thought I should have known better. Lots of shame attached to this, as I believed I let my Dad down.

The day after the huge Bar Mitzvah celebration, there was a brunch at my Aunt's place—an excuse for all of the extended family to get together. My cousin and I decided to go to the city pool. It was a hot day. My mother smiled and told us that it was fine if we could get someone to drive us. We ended up not getting into the pool because there was too long a wait. People were actually fainting in line from the hot sun. When we got back, my mother started screaming at me. She reminded me what the devil might have resembled. She said I should have stayed at my Aunt's luncheon. That was a little confusing for me as she said I could go swimming. We all jumped into the car and Dad drove us all home. My siblings were so quiet.

I found out years later that my mother had suffered a nervous breakdown in front of all of the extended family. Apparently, my Aunt was being stubborn about some-thing… and you don't become stubborn and disagree with my mother. This was a typical pattern in my relationship with my mother. She couldn't sustain being generous and kind for more than 24 hours without erupting.

I used to have countless dreams about my ability to fly like a bird. It felt so real and liberating. I never under-stood this as a child but when I grew older I figured it out. I felt trapped by my mother with no way out. I dreamt about being free from her judgments and anger.

I used to love going to summer camp for the same reason. I was the only child in our family who wanted to attend for two months every year. I did this for five years, from the age of 8 to 12. It was my escape. My way of get-ting away from all the pain and feelings of uselessness and incompetence. My counsellors at camp usually showed a lot of empathy and understanding, so it might have been one of the reasons I enjoyed camp life. I remember coming home from summer camp one year to find that my mother had made all my favourite foods. She was so happy because she knew this was one thing she couldn't screw up. It felt so good to see her in such a rejoicing mood. I felt safe, but cautious. Sadly, in keeping with the way things were, she went into a stark raving rage within five minutes of eating because someone had innocently said something she didn't like. I was so sad camp was over for another year.

You may have noticed that I've very rarely mentioned my Dad. Dad seemed invisible. We did not have a typical father/son relationship, as any son may want. My Dad never stood up to my Mom. He never wanted to attend any of my activities unless forced to by my mother. Yes, once in a while my mother realized that I needed my father in my life. My mother was quite intelligent and could be very observant, but not of her own actions. My Dad was totally immersed in his business. Dad was a doom and gloom type of guy. Every day he thought his business would fail. I felt his fear and it did nothing to help my confidence. I remember being out to lunch with Dad when I was in my late teens. At one point I called him "Dad" and he told me to be quiet. I couldn't understand, so I asked him what I had done wrong. He said, "There are women here and I don't want them to know I am married with kids". He also said that because of my age as his son, he didn't want people to think he was older than he looked. My Dad always looked about 20 years younger than his real age. I had no idea he thought that I could embarrass him. I remember that my younger brother used to get upset at Dad because he would talk about other women. My younger brother thought it was immature to talk to his son about his manly desires. It was difficult to perceive at this time in my life, but my Dad would later be a good friend, part of my support network as I grew older.

Just as I was finishing Grade 7, we moved from the town of Orillia. We had moved seven times by the time I was 11 years old, usually because my Dad made money on his house sales and purchases. My Mom also wanted to improve our status in life by living in bigger and better homes. I am not sure what effect that had on my life, but the lack of stability might be one consequence.

We moved to the City of Guelph where my Dad had set up a new business. I was never sure why he picked Guelph. Dad was not a big risk taker, but I have to give him credit for giving this a go. Dad seemed to have very little confidence, but he had self-assurance in the jewelry/ gift business and knew his stuff.

I was in Grade 8 when we moved to Guelph and I was in shock. In Orillia, we had one teacher per classroom for the duration of the year. In Guelph, you rotated and had many teachers. I was very confused by this. My mother had told me later in life, that I missed much of school and had issues with Montezuma's revenge (traveller's diarrhea). I don't remember this at all, but I do remember being very frightened. It didn't help that there was a Math teacher who used to physically abuse students and who, much like my mother, demanded respect. God help you if you didn't give it. He was on probation, and I was surprised that he was allowed to continue to teach because of his anger and the way in which he physically abused students. He once threw a student across the room and the student crashed into a bunch of desks. I was very surprised that the teacher wasn't fired. I guess adults turned a blind eye to a lot back then.

I had learned through my own experiences with my mother, that you don't mess with these people. You give total respect. If you did that, you might be safe. I had no problems with this teacher.

I struggled through that year and somehow managed to get on the Honours Roll. I didn't believe for one minute that I had done well enough to deserve this. My fellow students were in shock. I truly believe that my homeroom teacher saw me trying, felt empathy for me and somehow decided I needed a boost of confidence. I felt very uncomfortable receiving this award.

TWO

PUBERTY: WHY DIDN'T THEY HAVE VIAGRA BACK THEN?

SO THERE I was, in high school. I had defied the odds as I wasn't supposed to make it past Grade 8.

Something changed for me. I started thinking about girls. It was always in the forefront of my mind. It was the motivation for my happiness as I got up every morning. Today I would meet a girl. I believed that a girl could solve all my problems. A girl would love me and I would finally feel good about myself. I didn't meet any girls in Grade 9, as in my mind I wasn't a jock.

*I was just this invisible person
who walked through the halls.*

My mother often used to tell me that the one thing I had going for me was my looks. Although I realized that it didn't really help me if I had little confidence. I never gave up hopes of meeting the girl who would save me, but I didn't realize that I had a lot to learn. In Grade 10, when I was about 15 years old, a few things happened that had a major effect on my life.

I became focused on this girl across the street from my house. She was in Grade 9. When I was sitting outside my house, I started noticing her smiling at me from what I guess was her bedroom. She was in her bra looking down at me. Was this really happening? No, this couldn't be happening. I would grow more conscious of this as she would do this practically every day when I was outside. One day I saw her peering from her backyard at me and smiling. I decided to summon up the nerve to walk over to her, as she wouldn't stop staring at me. We started talking. Her older sister was also in the backyard but she ran into the house crying. I didn't understand why at that moment, but soon I found out that she had a crush on me and that her younger sister was stealing me away from her. The younger sister and I continued to talk. I could see she was quite interested in me. I wasn't sure how I felt about her. Apart from a young crush a girl had on me at camp, she seemed to be the first girl who showed a real interest in me (aside from her sister). I have to say for a Grade 9 girl, she had a well-developed woman's body. Guys would stare at her and I think my Dad was actually jealous of me. (On a side bar, I had noticed that my Dad seemed to lose all interest in Mom. And as time went on, it became more and more evident.)

Anyway, my first sexual experience was with this girl when I was 15. My family had moved out to the country not far away from Guelph. She came out to my house once when my family was away and we went to bed in my parents' room. The confusing part for me was that I pretty much had no sexual drive. I know she wanted intercourse, but I just wasn't interested. So we kissed and hugged, but that was about it. I couldn't get an erection. This bothered me immensely.

Was I gay? I didn't seem to have an interest in men. I ended up writing it off that I just wasn't attracted to her in that way. About a month or two later, I had attempted sexual relations with another girl… just a few times but again no erection. I wanted to and was interested this time, but to no avail. This started to bother me immensely and I ended up going to a psychiatrist (which I'll talk about later). There was no Viagra at the time and no computers available to look for erectile dysfunction cures.

Back to high school. I kept mostly to myself. I had one friend for quite a while and that was all. One day, for no reason (I didn't understand until recently), a jock started picking on me. Not by himself, but with a bunch of his followers who worshipped him. Of course, he was a bully. They would trap me about once a month in the halls and pull down my pants or take my shoes and socks. Sometimes they would just trip me in front of other people. The leader jock had everything going for him. He excelled scholastically, he was the captain of the football and the basketball teams, was good looking and he just oozed confidence. But there was something about him that seemed contrived. I couldn't figure out why he had to stoop so low as to pick on a skinny runt like me and needed five others to do it with.

I was never a follower. Perhaps that bothered him. I was Jewish, maybe he was anti-Semitic. Here I was, the cowardly-looking boy once again. Then an odd thing happened. As I was walking home one day, he caught up to me and started conversing like we were the best of friends. While he chatted he seemed like a little kid jabbering away and asking questions. I was on the alert all the time, but he was not hostile at all. As we walked past his house he waved goodbye and I continued home.

One day we were lining up for our booster shots in high school and it was the bully's turn. He was trembling, almost fainted and had tears in his eyes. He was carried out afterwards by one of his cronies. He looked at me as he was leaving and he reminded me of me. He looked like a scared little boy. This was my opportunity to laugh in his face in revenge for all the embarrassing things he had done to me. The thought crossed my mind, but I couldn't do it. I only showed empathy. He never touched me again.

Unfortunately, both my sexual issues and my encounter with this bully damaged me for years to come. It was only recently that the bully issue began to make sense. I represented everything that frightened him… his fear of being a "nobody" and looking weak. No wonder the booster shot episode must have been difficult for him. I believe that is why he had to excel at everything he did. Do I know for sure? No, but the thought brought me peace.

I was barely making it in school and the most significant development to date happened to me when I was 18 years old in my last year of High School. I finally met (who I thought was) the girl who would save me from my own insecurities. She had a crush on me and wanted to meet me. She had blond hair, was fairly slim, had freckles that I loved and she was rather reserved. I finally worked up the nerve to ask her out.

Through this relationship, I started to understand how deeply insecure I really was. To this day, she doesn't know this. I would always show up late on purpose, act aloof, sort of like I could take or leave the relationship. My mother had brainwashed me to believe that people were out to take advantage of me and if I showed that I cared, I'd be doomed. So out of fear and at the risk of embarrassment, I followed my Mom's lead. The problem was, I wasn't being me. I was extremely attracted to her and wanted to be with her every minute of every day. It was so difficult to keep up this pretense.

One day it backfired on me. I was going to university and she was in Grade 12. I kept on suggesting to her that university would be exciting and that I couldn't wait to start. That I was looking forward to having a lot more freedom from parents, etc. I made no mention of missing her or whether I would come back to visit her. I was attempting to make her jealous. Mistakenly clinging onto my mother's beliefs that my dismissive behaviour would make her want me more.

The opposite happened. To avoid feeling rejected, (she told me these thoughts many years later) she decided to find someone else and ended up marrying him. I was such a jerk. I was heartbroken. When she told me it was over between us, I cried like a little baby in front of her. I was hurting so very much that when I drove away, I decided to block the whole thing out of my mind. I found instant relief, which wasn't a healthy way to deal with deep emotions. I knew that, but didn't care. I never thought about her again except for one incident a couple months later. I noticed her new boyfriend at a bar and started to get in his face, I wanted to fight him, but my friends tore me away. He could have wiped the floor with me, but he actually seemed like a decent guy and let me be. I was still quite upset as I had lost the one thing that seemed to rescue me from my low self- esteem. I had to let it go and I did.

During the ten months that my girlfriend and I had been together, we did a lot of kissing and touching, but no intercourse took place. We finally had an opportunity. For some reason, I was feeling as if she wasn't as interested in me as she used to be, but I could tell she really wanted to go to bed with me. I failed miserably. I couldn't get an erection and I craved it so badly. I wanted to love her like I had never loved anyone before. I felt regretful afterwards, but she was very kind and told me that it really didn't matter. For sure it did to me. It was so devastating. I couldn't know at the time, but my high school girlfriend and I were not done.

THREE

YOUNG ADULT STUDENT – I HAD
NO IDEA WHAT I WAS DOING

WELL, I FINALLY started university. The guy who would never make it past Grade 8, and was supposedly mentally handicapped. I think sometimes that maybe my drive to fight against my "incorrectly diagnosed destiny" is what kept me motivated and moving forward. There was good and bad that came from this. The good will become obvious later. Unfortunately, the bad meant that I had trouble ever relaxing. I felt I had to continue to run away from the belief that I was a failure and not good enough.

I started off in University by studying Accounting and

it wasn't my calling. I was totally confused about what I wanted to do. I just knew, that like my siblings, I had to attend university. I had no idea what subject I was interested in. My Mom had told me to get involved in business. She said that my older brother and sister were in the Social Sciences and would never make good money... and therefore would never be successful. For her, that was what life was all about. You must show success financially. She inferred that my two eldest siblings were losers. I decided to listen to her because I felt that if I succeeded where my siblings wouldn't, I would become confident and secure. One of the biggest mistakes I ever made. My older brother became a successful university Professor with tenure and did very well. My sister became a therapist in Florida and married a doctor. I am sure you'd appreciate that my Jewish mother couldn't have been happier for my sister. But the point here is my mother had been mistaken about the careers of my siblings. They both did well, both scholastically and financially, but possibly not good enough for her.

Being in university, I decided to leave home and live in residence.

I felt like I was a person who had just been exonerated from prison and had a new lease on life.

Miracles do happen. I could fly like a bird.

It wasn't long after this that my parents divorced. It meant very little to me as I knew they weren't happy. Dad wanted his freedom.

In my first year of university at Waterloo Luthren, (so

it was called at the time), I lived in an all-male residence. It was partying 24/7. The hallways wreaked of marijuana and hash. I had a roommate who was about 6 foot 4, heavy-set, a crazy, loud-mouthed guy. He really didn't like me much, but that turned around after a while. Thank God he went home on weekends. I barely made it through my first year at university, as I really didn't like my course of studies. In fact, the whole male residence had failed the Accounting course except for three of us... or so I was told.

During my year at Lutheran, I'd met a woman and it was the first time I actually had sexual intercourse. I wasn't a master at it, but I was good enough. I would still have my moments when I couldn't perform.

I decided to transfer to Guelph where there was an Honours Bachelor of Commerce degree specializing in Hotel and Food Administration.

I stopped seeing the woman at Lutheran. I had a habit of liking certain women for a limited amount of time and then I would break up with them. Possibly a fear of getting too close and then being rejected. I know this related back to my mother and her misguided beliefs... and possibly the experience I had with my girlfriend who broke my heart in Grade 13.

Before I transferred over to Guelph, I had to have an initial meeting with the Department Head. He took one look at me and gasped. I had lots of hair, styled like an afro, dirty clothes, and dusty construction boots as I'd had just got off work from summer road construction. He was extremely conservative. He asked me how I'd managed to get into this class and in a derogatory manner he said, "You can't walk around my department like this". I got quite defensive with the old coot. I told him I had no financial aid and the only way I could make enough money was to work as much as I could during the summer. I couldn't afford to take time off work to change as I was also living on my own. He calmed down a little.

I remember the first day in class when most of the men came in with briefcases and wearing suits. I had faded (but clean) jeans, and was still sporting the afro and a knapsack. I wondered if I'd made a mistake making this course a career choice. I was starting to believe I had. I wanted some sort of University degree in business so that I could prove I wasn't a failure and I was keeping up with my siblings. No wonder I was so unhappy.

I was striving to find something to escape my feelings of low self-esteem, instead of striving to find something that excited me and gave me purpose.

I had very little interest in the course as I progressed. I skipped lots of classes. I was a rebel. I had always behaved myself through school up until now. No doubt, with this move to Guelph University, my decisions in life were getting me down. Deep inside I was angry about my situation, but at the time I couldn't figure out what was happening to me.

Aside from my screwed up school choice, I was having a great time partying quite a bit. I found myself in a situation where these two girls, who were friends, both liked me. One night after a university dance they wanted me to come back to their rooms. I picked the girl who didn't have a boyfriend. She was actually quite dominating, and of course, I couldn't get an erection. I don't think she was used to that and she kept on saying, "c'mon, get it up." Well, that didn't help. I left feeling quite shameful. Anyway, I continued seeing her and I managed to become a little more adequate, but she was not a very loving soul. Christmas break was coming up and I asked her if I could visit her at her home. Why I wanted to do this, I'll never know. A glutton for punishment I guess.

My friend's girlfriend and my girlfriend (and I use the term "my girlfriend" loosely) lived in the same town and we all went to a club together. We were sitting down and having drinks and I wasn't completely sure at the time, but I think a guy came up to her and they started necking. My friend confirmed it and said, "David let's leave". I felt too ashamed to get up and go. They were probably kissing for about ten minutes. I felt like a total jerk. Too afraid to get up and hit the guy, as my cowardice showed itself again, I just sat there. Was it worth fighting for this girl? Well we ended up going back to her place and she told me to get lost. I don't know if I ever felt any lower in my life.

I finally decided to see a psychiatrist in Toronto as I was at the end of my tether. Why did I continue to punish myself by dating girls who didn't appreciate me, and dropping the girls who did? At the time, I felt my experience with this psychiatrist was a big mistake. Or maybe it wasn't, and perhaps I had to go through this.

Back then, psychiatry was definitely different than today. The man I initially met with in Toronto asked me a number of questions. He was quite abrupt and did zilch to make me feel at all comfortable. He had a sour look on his face, wore dark-rimmed glasses and had a balding head. He seemed extremely angry. I felt like a criminal. At one point he said, "when did you start masturbating?" I thought about it and finally said, "at about 18 or 19." He said that was way too old and asked why I didn't start earlier. I replied that I wasn't sure. I didn't know it was unusual to only start masturbating in my late teens. I must admit that the first few times I discovered masturbation I felt so guilty, so shameful. It was devastating. But soon the amazing feeling superseded the guilt and I realized what I had been missing out on.

Masturbation is said to be so normal, but the hang-ups surrounding this and sex are amazing.

The psychiatrist decided to set me up with a child psychiatrist. I guess he thought I had to look at my early years to find answers to my issues. I was introduced to my psychiatrist. A short man, maybe about 5'4" and heavy-set. He was quite wrinkled and seemed to wear a hairpiece (but I wasn't 100 % sure about that). Maybe he just dyed his hair. He lived at home with his mother.

I can't remember all the conversations I had with him, but I recall that he fell asleep on several occasions. I think I kept on repeating the same frustrating stuff about my family in every session. I guess he was bored. I had to get over a hump, but he did nothing to help me work through my demons. He just listened. Well, sometimes he wasn't even listening.

Finally, at one point, after about a year and maybe 20 sessions, I said something that sent him into shock. It was so difficult for me to say this. I mentioned that I was a little confused about my manhood. That maybe I was supposed to be a woman (the whole chromosome mix up thing). Back then you didn't say those things. (How the concept of "normal" has changed over the years.) He sat upright in his chair and said in an anxious tone, "There must be something wrong with you". Oh, I said, "Thanks for being so understanding". I was pissed. This coming from a man with a hairpiece, who lived with his mother at the age of 45 or 50 years old and who had never been married. Yes, I had judgments. I left and never went back.

He would call me at home and pleaded with me to see him again because he believed that I needed help. His method wasn't the way to get me back. I refused. This was the last time I saw a shrink or anyone close to that until much later in my life.

The masculinity thing was something I wrestled with for many years. I just couldn't understand why I couldn't get aroused with a woman. Let me correct that. I could get aroused by a woman—I just couldn't get, but mostly hold an erection.

As you can imagine I never brought this up with any-one again, as it was obviously very embarrassing. It was a personal issue that I battled with privately. I didn't want to seem abnormal by discussing this with anybody. I have a feeling most men are too ashamed to discuss these matters. I did wonder where this issue stemmed from. I had a few theories on this.

Number 1: Was it related to my sister? From my perspective (and my perspective only), I always thought my sister had it the easiest. It was safe being a female in the family. She seemed to have an easy life. On a side note, I remember when I was around seven years old, my Dad had bought my sister a pair of earrings. I was hurt as he didn't get me anything. I told my Dad to buy me a pair. I guess he talked about it with Mom. Their belief was possibly that if he bought me a pair I would realize it wasn't about the earrings. He brought them home. I put them on for about five minutes and took them off. I have no idea what happened to them after that. I can only suspect my parents were right that I felt left out and wanted to be as important and loved as my sister or I was beginning a new trend in men wearing earrings.

Number 2: Did my mother's constant abuse make it difficult for me to trust women?

Number 3: Was I just a late bloomer and immature in that area?

Number 4: Was it related to the unnecessary and terrifying appendix surgery that my Mom forced on me when she said she would "cut it out"?

Number 5: Or was it just my own confusion and unhappiness about my life situation?

I think it was a combination of all of the above, and other things I might not even be aware of. My intentions were to continue to work through this.

At some point in my life, I became much more self-assured in certain areas. The sexual problem was still there but I was a man and there was no more confusion with this.

FOUR

SINGLE POST-STUDENT YEARS: I WAS FREE OR WAS I? ARE WE EVER TOTALLY FREE?

I TRUDGED THROUGH UNIVERSITY and got my degree. What do you know? The mentally handicapped guy was still moving forward. I felt so free in my first few months after being finished with my education. No teachers, no studying, no living off macaroni and wieners. I was so happy and relieved.

I tried to find jobs in the Hotel and Food Industry even though I had little interest in the field. I was living in Guelph and knew I had to move to Toronto to get my career started. Toronto was a large city with lots of opportunities. Guelph was nice and safe, but there was nowhere for me to work. It was a difficult decision. I had been unemployed for about a year and got compensation from the government as I had worked every summer for about four months while in University. It seemed like macaroni and wieners were still on the menu.

Finally I got an opportunity in London, Ontario through my parents. A possible management career in insurance. I showed up for the interview with lots of time to spare and my interviewer said it was a sure thing. I had the job opening. He told me that I'd just have to complete a type of personality test as a formality. I was ecstatic that I'd finally be earning an income to support myself. So I completed the test, went back after lunch, and met the interviewer. He had this horrific look on his face. His eyes were wide open and he seemed quite disappointed. He said, "I am sorry, I can't hire you". I said, "What is the problem? You said it was a sure thing". He said "this test says you have some crazy thoughts". I begged him to give me a chance. He said, "I just can't". I couldn't figure out what I had said in the test that sent him into shock. I was devastated.

When would I get a break? Maybe I had taken the test too literally when it said "be as honest as possible". Maybe I was too honest. My interpretation of normal wasn't being accepted yet. But looking back on it, it probably was for the best as I wasn't suited to a desk job shuffling paper-work. At the time I only saw myself as a total loser and quite abnormal.

While I was stuck in Guelph, waiting for some other job to come along, I met a woman. I think she was fairly uneducated and lived at home. She had a 5-year-old child and worked full time. She was 20 years old. She wasn't matured at expressing herself, was very quiet, and for some reason I was quite attracted to her. Maybe it was the long blond hair. Or perhaps it was desperation to find the ulti-mate woman. At first she really enjoyed being with me. Unfortunately, she always wanted to hang out at bars. I wasn't crazy about this as I wasn't a big drinker and she was quite the flirt. Also it wasn't a great place to have intelligent conversations. At one of these bars a friend of hers came up to her, looked at me and said, "I see you have a Latin Lover." She said, "Not quite" and laughed. Yes, the sexual problems were still there. As time went on, I allowed her to take charge of the relationship. I would go to pick her up at her parents' house and she wouldn't be there. The father used to laugh at me when I came to the door. Once I got so desperate that I parked a street over and waited to see if she came back to her house with someone else. For some silly reason, I couldn't resist her, no matter how badly she treated me. Despite this, I was being quite the gentleman with her and I guess she wasn't used to being respected at that level. I couldn't understand why I would want to be with someone who treated me so miserably. This pattern had happened before.

I asked my older brother about this destructive pattern of mine. He suggested to me that there would come a time when you would stoop so low… literally crawling on your stomach… and only then would you have had enough. I wished that time would come. It was one of the first occa-sions that my brother was empathetic with me and it felt good. Well his advice came to pass.

I had an interview in Toronto and landed a job. I phoned my girlfriend and said I needed to see her. I went over to her house and she laughed saying, "What do you want now?" I said, "I can't take this anymore. I've allowed you to treat me like a patsy and I have to tell you that I feel quite good about ending this. There is no debate." She started to sob and begged me to stay. Her reaction made no sense to me whatsoever. I left and never looked back. I felt like a million bucks and my self-esteem was resurrected for the time being.

Before I landed my first job in Toronto, I had been interviewed for a management position in Yorkville with the General Manager of an up and coming restaurant chain. I must have had about eight interviews with this fellow and I started getting frustrated and pissed at him. This was a low-level, entry position in a fairly new company. I needed money and I needed a job. I thought it was rude of him to just keep me on the sidelines. In the final interview, I was belligerent and he said, "Well with this type of attitude I can't see hiring you". I said "exactly" and left. I decided to take a job with an owner of a company who had only three restaurants and he had an interest in large expansion. I started at the minimum wage, which was $2.35 an hour, even though I had just received an Honours university degree. In my defense, the economy in 1971 was in a deep recession at the time and you took what you could get. I had a new small car, a bachelor apartment and some money left over at the end of each month. How things have changed economically over the years. My boss once came up to me and asked if I wanted a raise. I said,

"No, I'm fine". I look back at this now and laugh. This subservient attitude of mine changed in the future.

Well, the company did start to expand and ended up growing to 50 stores and then the company bought another company. Through time and experience, I had been promoted to Director of Operations. I was making good money and the benefits were excellent.

The only hitch was that I personally found the owner very difficult to work for. Probably, because like my mother, he would fly into a rage when least expected. I am sure he felt it was warranted. Why did I always find myself in relationships with many of my girlfriends, teachers, schoolyard bullies, bosses – who were very similar to my mother in her ability to make me feel worthless?

On the other hand, although I was quite good at my job, I could also be effective at making people feel unworthy. Constantly taking a defensive position, I could be quite unsympathetic and rude with my staff. I would lose my temper, yell at them and behave quite unreasonably sometimes. Was my behaviour warranted? This behaviour is never ever warranted. I should have found another way, but at the time I was too immature and insecure. Were my staff little angels? Not at all, but there were other ways to deal with staff issues.

I am quite regretful about my way of being back then.
I was turning into my mother.

I did improve much later in life when I had an "awakening". We'll get to that later.

For a while, being the Director of Operations was quite thrilling for me, but as time went on it lost its luster. I was failing. I was supposed to be famous, or a brilliant, rich, businessman. I was none of these. I did well, but nothing close to my expectations (or should I say my mother's). I should also mention, that my uncles and aunts were mostly rich and successful. When I say rich, I mean *rich*! I once chatted to my one uncle who had approximately $80 million in the bank at the time. I asked him, "Is there anything that you regret about your life?" He said, "Yeah, see that guy over there?" pointing to one of my other uncles. "He said he has $100 million. I want more than him." Did they have that much? I don't know but here I was, with my measly job and my measly house... feeling like a complete failure. Comparing ourselves to others is common but unhealthy as it lowers our self- esteem.

It would take many years of personal, inner work for me to realize how skewed my thinking was.

The beliefs that had been ingrained in me were self-destructive and I had to free myself of them in order to find peace, basic contentment and feel good about myself.

During my career as Director of Operations, two significant developments occurred in my relationship with my mother.

I cut her off and refused to have anything to do with her for two years. I had had enough of her bullshit. I felt good about this at first, but at some point it niggled away at me. I started to feel very guilty, so I decided to work myself back into her life very slowly. Cutting off is not a healthy solution. It turned out that she was never able to forgive me for abandoning her. I mean never. I remember how, years later, she gave my one brother a piano, the other brother $5,000, and her best silverware went to my sister. I received nothing. She'd also decided that she wanted me cut out of her will, but my oldest brother wouldn't allow it. At one point, my older brother told me that he'd respected my decision to stand up to our mother. He said he could never do it. I felt very good about this. Maybe he didn't realize that he had also stood up to Mom and went against her wishes, by not agreeing to cut me off from any inheritance.

Secondly, my mother fell ill and was moved permanently to a facility called Bay Crest. She lay in a bed for over 17 years. During the first years, she refused to exercise. My self-diagnosis was that she became so depressed that she couldn't function anymore. This wasn't entirely correct. She had seen psychiatrists for many years, but nothing seemed to help. The running joke in our family was that Mom would only go to psychiatrists who would agree with everything she said, and would never dare challenge her!

It was sad watching her lie in her hospital bed with the smell of urine permeating the room, her teeth falling out and her legs turning into small twigs.

In the final analysis, it seemed the cause of her demise was a couple of issues. She'd had a myelogram on her back, which my younger brother said the doctors screwed up and which left her with constant back pain. Secondly, she had CMT which I will discuss shortly. Finally, she also suffered from depression. In all likelihood, I'd say it was the physical issues that kept her in depression, however she'd been depressed as long as I knew her. She simply gave up. I did notice that at some point I started to forgive her. But it wasn't until now, as I sit writing this book, that I realize I am totally at peace with her. I feel so much empathy for her and what seems like an unhappy life.

As time went on, my mother somehow managed to break her jaw. They put a cast around her chin and head so she wouldn't move her jaw. She was temporarily put into a ward instead of her private room and she screamed consistently. There was nothing else anyone could do until the jaw healed. She ended up dying there all alone. That, in itself, was quite unfortunate. I questioned my feelings at the time and for the most part I felt overwhelming relief. Yes, I did have some empathy for her at the time—but mostly it was for me. Possibly selfish. But now I could stop being overshadowed and cowered by the consistent criticism she directed at me (and others). For the most part, I held her responsible for my low self-esteem issues. However, I'd subsequently learned that I needed to move past that thinking, or I'd be a victim for life.

I also had unfortunate thoughts about my brothers. They had bonded and seemed to love being with each other. I remember going to Ottawa where they were both living. I felt totally ignored. My brothers walked with each other, talked with each other and hardly said a word to me. (These feelings of being left out reared themselves in illogical ways in my 60s… which I'll get to later). From my perspective (and my perspective only), my older brother was simply irritated with me, and my youngest brother found me embarrassing.

It would take me until later in life to understand that if my thoughts about my brothers were true, these would be their issues and not mine. These feelings didn't make me a bad person, nor did it say anything bad about them if they didn't like having conversations with me. What I started to understand is that, just because I am a brother, it doesn't mean that we'll get along with each other.

I can't force anyone to like me. And in order to be liked, I won't change my way of being so much that I sacrifice my own personality.

I would email my siblings regularly later in life, wanting to keep the connection. If any of them weren't interested, they knew they had choices. None of them ever wrote and said they were *not* interested in hearing from me. Maybe they were just being polite. But I will say this… I believe each one of them would be there for me if I needed them. That's my perception anyway. I would also be there for them. I know so many families where this is not true.

FIVE

MARRIED: MY ATTEMPT AT BEING NORMAL

I EVENTUALLY GOT MARRIED at around 30. I remember ramping up for a long distance hard run before our marriage. I guess I wasn't sure if the marriage was right for either one of us, but part of me thought this was the natural progression of life and it is what people do. There I was, following 'normal'.

It wasn't necessarily right for me, but at the time it was what was done to be 'accepted' in society. My wife-to-be had two kids of her own, which caused some parenting issues as is common with most step-parents and step-kids. My wife was pretty good with me about handling her kids. She let me correct them when they made mistakes or were just being teens. But step-families definitely have their struggles and challenges.

I wanted kids of our own, so we went ahead and had two daughters.

One of my girls was diagnosed with Charcot Marie Toothe disease (CMT). CMT, for the most part, affects the lower legs, feet, arms and hands. I want to mention at this time, that the doctors didn't diagnose my mother with CMT when she was lying in the nursing home. CMT was not widely-known in the medical world then, but in hindsight, I'm convinced that she suffered from it too as somehow it was passed on, and she showed all the symptoms of it. To this day, knowledge of this disease is still not widely recognized.

How did we realize our daughter had this disease? My daughter would walk to school every day and once she came back with a broken foot, just from walking. At first, we just thought that something we didn't understand had happened… a fluke of some sort… a mystery of the universe. The foot cured and then it happened again. My wife suggested we take her to see a specialist. They ran some tests and then asked me to come in. They induced both my daughter and me with shocks to test our nervous systems. We responded very slowly to shock. Most people would feel the shock right away, we didn't. They diagnosed both my daughter and me with CMT. I wondered why I had not shown the symptoms that my daughter had shown. Although, remember the comment about me 'marching' to school? He was onto something. Could this explain why I was never as talented as my siblings were on the piano, or other musical instruments? The doctors suggested that I simply had a mild case of CMT. I used to sprain my foot constantly when I was a kid, but I never thought any more about it.

My daughter suffers greatly from the CMT and has constant foot operations. She can barely walk at times. Her last operation consisted of implanting seven screws. My younger daughter was also diagnosed with the disease but it seems to be milder, although she has broken her foot 3 times in the past 8 years. Would I still have had kids regardless of this CMT knowledge? Probably. But I can't know for sure unless I'd been told about this disease before I had kids. I love my kids. It would have been an unfortunate blunder if I'd decided not to have them.

Interesting how people's lives could potentially change substantially if they had certain bits of physical information about themselves beforehand. I'm sure at some point medical advances will mean that people will be diagnosed with diseases immediately at birth – maybe even before.

I remember once seeing my doctor and saying to him, "If only I didn't have CMT. I had so much energy and drive. I could have been a great runner or a great musician, as I had a great passion for it." He said something to me that resonated in my very soul. He said compassionately (with some forcefulness), "But you do". I always saw this fellow as a very wise man. He had an amazing following and he was right. I did have CMT so what was the point of hankering after what couldn't be? Why try to be the best at something where you are already hampered—making it even more difficult to achieve? That would be me. Finding things that would ensure my failure.

When my daughters were very young, one wanted to get physically close to others and loved to hug at a very young age, whereas the other seemed quite withdrawn, sad, yet serious… that was my perception. The serious one never wanted to do anything with me. I would ask her to go for a walk, and she would refuse. I would ask her to grab an ice cream with me, and she would refuse. I would suggest that we go for a drive, and she would refuse. I had believed that daughters just loved their Daddies, but she was a definite exception. Here I was, once again being rejected. Then one night at the age of around four, she came upstairs in her cute little bathrobe and slippers. She noticed that I was watching a movie. One of my favourite actors back then was Arnold Schwarzenegger. I loved his action movies and how he was always the hero. She sat beside me on the couch (which was in itself quite unexpected) and stayed through the whole movie. I thought to myself, "what four-year-old girl likes Schwarzenegger movies?" I was worried about the violence, and discussed the subject with my wife, but she was just so immersed in the movie that I didn't know how to restrict her from watching. And so it happened that whenever I was watching Schwarzenegger, she would drop everything she was doing and sit beside me on the couch with total concentration on her face. An interesting way to bond with my four-year-old daughter, but I would take what I could get.

I saw my ex-wife and me as quite dysfunctional. We argued almost every day. Ask us at the time who was to blame, and we would both have blamed the other… Looking back at it now, I learned how we both contributed to the breakdown of the marriage. I'll admit I could be a hot head and defensive. I made the mistake of believing I was rescuing her at first. I wanted to be the white knight in life. When I met her, she owed money and was living as a single mom in what I think was a subsidized townhouse. If she looked up to me, I believed it would help my self-esteem issues. I wanted thankfulness and appreciation from her, but that didn't last past the first year. We couldn't and wouldn't take responsibility for ourselves. I thought I was trying, but deep down inside I thought she was mostly responsible. Thoughts aren't facts.

My biggest regret was watching my little kids suffer… plugging their ears when we fought. It was so unfair. So unfair. I believe it did irrefutable psychological damage to our kids, possibly one more than the other. That didn't mean it was so, but it was what I believed.

My other huge regret was that I didn't spend enough time with the kids. My wife had them singing and dancing the bulk of their free time. I remember one period when I had sold a business of mine and was without work for a number of months. I had time to spend with the kids. I would take them to the bus every day and help them with homework questions. Both my daughters went from getting C's at school to straight A's. They seemed to be much happier and I wish I had spent less time worrying about myself, and more time being with my children.

Our marriage lasted for 17 years. About two years before we separated, I had an affair. It only lasted for a month, as I felt guilty every day. I wanted loving, with no judgments so badly, but I wasn't good at betraying my wife no matter how difficult things were between us. However, I did decide that I had to leave our relationship. The night before I was supposed to leave, my daughter and my wife were lying in bed with me. They were quite upset. I couldn't do it. I couldn't leave. We had tried couples counselling on a few different occasions, but for the most part my wife seemed to feel quite uncomfortable with the process. I never understood why and she never really explained the reason. I stayed for two more years. Lived in another part of the house for a year and then left.

This was the beginning of a difficult transition for me, and the beginning of a new life.

SIX

ONE OF MY CRAZY TIMES: ARE WE LEARNING YET?

I MOVED TO A bachelor apartment in downtown Toronto as I couldn't find anything near my family. I was lost. The owner of the company I was with at the time fired me. I had never been fired before. If it was any consolation, he wanted to rehire me six months later. I would have nothing to do with it.

So here I was… separated, without my kids, and with no job.

I disliked my choice of career, but in my mid-forties, I hardly had the skills to do anything else. I remember wandering around in a fog for six months. I was in a panic and could see myself ending my life. I remember attending a Bar Mitzvah wearing a soiled shirt and pants that kept falling down because I hadn't worn a belt. I was usually quite conscious of my dress, but no more. Nothing seemed to matter. I felt drugged.

I was later told that my cousin had secretly set me up with someone at the event. I never realized this was happening nor was I conscious of anything else around me.

I went through a phase where I hadn't slept for seven nights in a row… not for one hour. I started hallucinating. During that weekend, I brought the kids down to my place and as I was driving I kept imagining that cars were going to crash into me. After having the kids for the weekend, I told my ex-wife that I couldn't drive them back. I believed I would cause them to be involved in an accident. She came and picked them up. Not very often (for good reason), but on that occasion my wife had empathy for me. It felt good.

I went to a walk-in clinic to acquire a prescription for sleeping pills and I felt relieved that I would finally get some sleep, but they didn't help at all. I came to the conclusion (I don't know why) that I had to get out of my apartment and away from Toronto. I went to my older brother's house in Guelph. He wasn't the brother I remembered from when I was a kid. He seemed to have done some real growing up in the number of years I hadn't seen him. He offered me a herbal sedative called Valerian Root. I took it and could immediately feel a sense of calmness coming over me. My brother was very supportive to me during this time and truly empathetic. I slept for five hours. I felt so much better after being sleep-deprived for a straight week.

I came to the conclusion that we all need a close friend, or sibling, just someone who will be there for us when we're suffering.

My cousin wanted to set me up for counselling with a therapist named Jane. I refused and said, "not in a million years!" I clearly remembered my unpleasant experiences in my 20s with the two therapists. I was feeling more and more hopeless. I had no job and, in general, my life situation was at its' lowest.

I finally agreed to reach out for help. I wasn't capable of solving this situation on my own and my support system couldn't help me through this. I believed I was suffering from a breakdown. When I first met Jane, I was ignorant and pessimistic. But that didn't last long. I had met someone who was a God-send. She was gentle and soothed me with her words. Until then (as you know) I had believed that people were untrustworthy and that God was only interested in punishing people for their mistakes. Jane taught me another way with an introduction to "A Course of Miracles". She asked me to join her and her husband's therapy group. I was a little reluctant, but I agreed. I attended every week for three years.

During this time, I acquired a job back at my original company. I was recruited at a lower position, but I didn't care. I was so thankful that they had allowed me to work for them. I was thrilled that I had a job, I could once again pay my bills, and get back on my feet. The company also gave me Tuesdays off to attend my spiritual group, as it was a whole day experience. It came to pass that they promoted me back to my original position as Director of Operations.

My Dad loaned me some money to buy a nice townhouse and this allowed me to move out of my small bachelor apartment in Toronto. I was starting to see things in another light. Relief came over me. The spiritual group, the company, and my Dad were on my side.

I learned to lean on others when I needed to and felt comfortable about exposing my vulnerability.

This was going against my mother's philosophy that you never show weakness.

My eldest daughter came and lived with me in my Newmarket townhouse. She was finished with school for the time being. I was starting to like my life. Things weren't perfect, but they were so much more hopeful.

I did hear about Dad complaining to others that he needed the money he had loaned to me and that he hated that I had put him in that position. I felt guilty hearing this from others. When I'd originally asked him for help, he didn't even hesitate. "No problem at all. Anything to help my kids," he said. I suggested a payment plan and he told me not to worry about it. He actually didn't need the money, but my Dad had a way of convincing others he was broke when he wasn't. I recall one of my cousins once asking me if it was true that my Dad was broke, and that if he was I should lend him some money. I said, "Absolutely not, he has over a million dollars in the bank". This knowledge Dad had shared with me grudgingly.

Regardless, one of the aunts left Dad some money in her will believing he was penniless.

I ended up finding a way to pay him back right away…
not because he needed it, but because he thought he needed
it. I didn't want to think I was the cause of his misery, even
if I wasn't.

SEVEN

LIGHT AT THE END OF THE TUNNEL: WITH SOME FLICKERS

AT SOME POINT, Jane had asked me if I wanted to get my Master's therapist's degree. She was associated with a group named *Clearminds Toronto chapter*, who were connected to a university in the States. I wasn't crazy about schooling as I'd had nightmares about ever having to deal with deadlines and exams again after I had finished university, but I thought this was an opportunity I couldn't pass up. I had finally found what I thought was my calling. At 48 years old, after decades of feeling lost and frustrated, I knew where I belonged. I ended up passing the course with

Honours and scored an "A" on my thesis. I was now a therapist. I excelled and felt confident for the first time in my life.

Anyone and everyone will excel if they can find their real calling… the work that gives them purpose.

My only indiscretion during this time was my "need" (not a want), to still have women in my life. I needed them to make me whole. By this time Viagra was available. I went from making so-so love to becoming a total stud. I could have sex and feel quite confident and relaxed. I went out with lots of women and tried to make up for a life of total sexual frustration. It was like I had to make up for past inadequacies.

I am sure some of you are able to identify with my situation (even if you have never spoken of it before). I felt I had been dealt a lousy deck struggling so much with relaxing and enjoying sex. I was not taking advantage of women just to have sex. Well, maybe it could be seen that way by some… but most of the women I met didn't want a long-standing relationship at the time. So I guess I am absolved of my sins to some degree.

I had become mostly honest and open about my inadequacies with others. Up until then, I had kept these parts hidden. I was so afraid that I'd be laughed at and ridiculed, but it didn't seem to matter anymore. I thought of it this way… if someone wasn't going to like me because of a certain trait of mine, I'd rather find out at the beginning of the relationship instead of later on. It's difficult to apply this thinking when you really like someone.

If you shared your innermost self with them, could it spell the end of the relationship? On the other hand, if someone of interest can't handle what you tell them, do you really want to be with them?

There was one place I wasn't totally honest. If I went out with a woman and I thought there might be a chance of having sex, I would pop a blue pill just in case. As I'd mentioned, I wanted to project this air of being a total stud. I could hardly do this if I had to say, "just hold on while I pop a Viagra pill and then we have to wait for about 30 minutes". Seems to take away from the whole experience. If I saw a woman more than once, I would let go of my stud secret. I didn't see a lot of women more than once.

There came a point in my life when I finally decided to grow up. I started to lose interest in all the dating and sex. Internet dating had had its 15 minutes of fame with me and I wanted a relationship. Someone I could wake up with. Someone who would celebrate special occasions with me. Someone I could share my achievements with. Someone I could be there for, to support their life and goals. I wanted a connection.

From the beginning of my exploration into the internet dating world, a woman called Dianne had caught my eye—but for some reason, I had never contacted her. I decided to connect with her just before I disappeared from the scene altogether.

Well, I guess you can imagine the outcome. We started going out. The timing was right and I think we all know how important timing is. I was attracted to her instantly and I was pretty sure that she was interested in me. She had red hair, freckles and knew how to be thrifty with her money. Three of my favourites. She also had a way of walking, as if she had taken modelling courses (which I later found out she had).

We had been going out for three months and everything seemed comfortable. It seemed meant to be. Then something happened. My old girlfriend from high school (who I was crushed by and who I had liked immensely), emailed me after all these years. She had left her husband. We started emailing each other. She confessed that she had always loved me and that she had broken off with me to avoid being hurt. She had thought since I was leaving for university I would reject her first.

We decided to meet. I was so confused. I had just met the best woman I had known, but I remembered how much I had liked my high school sweetheart. I was hiding this from Dianne.

Well, one day when Dianne was visiting, I had left my laptop open. She saw all this online. She looked at me with disbelief. "How could you?! We're so close and I see this?" She wasn't angry, just confused. I tried to explain how confused I was. I did not want to lose Dianne. She was everything to me. The final touch to a better life.

I made a decision not to see my high school flame and ended it. My high school sweetheart was confused about my thinking, but I looked at it as a teenage fantasy resurrected. I had changed so much. I am sure she had as well. I couldn't take the chance. I came to terms with it and stayed with Dianne.

The most redeemable thing about Dianne, aside from her courage, her intelligence and her looks, was her capacity to forgive. This, above all, was missing in my life from day one. I put my knee down on the patio of Starbucks and asked her to marry me. Maybe cheesy, but it was one of our favourite places at the time.

We married within the year. I must admit, when we woke up the day after the wedding, we both looked at each other feeling a little uncomfortable. Had we really done this? The awkward feeling didn't last long. Thank God. During the 15 years we have been together, I have never looked at another woman or had any feelings for another woman.

I am a firm believer that people who are attracted to each other have similar core values. Let me explain. Dianne had a fairly rough childhood. She was the only female in a family of four kids. Her brothers used to tease her quite regularly and her parents always felt sorry for her. When she was in her late twenties, she became a severe alcoholic. She is not embarrassed to share this information today. She hasn't had a drink in almost 34 years as she quit when she was 31. To this day, she doesn't want anyone feeling sorry for her.

Her brothers respect her now, as she is quite a strong woman. She had turned her life around, became an accountant and was employed as a Controller for a very lucrative, long-term company. It takes a lot of guts and willpower to stop an addiction, but she did it. She didn't see it as such a brave feat as I did. The bottom line here is that both Dianne and I had struggled against difficult odds and had experienced similar sibling issues. Our core values and the way we saw the world were in sync. We understood each other.

As time went on I continued on my path as a part-time therapist and I practiced in the evenings. I eventually gave up my full-time job as a Director of Operations and stopped commuting from Guelph to Toronto every day. I had little choice as I felt chest pains, had a panic attack and fainted a couple of times. It was the best decision I could ever have made. My practice became successful and grew to thirty clients a week. All my pains and other issues disappeared for the time being.

However, due to all the stress I subjected myself to, commuting to Toronto at 5.30 a.m. every morning to perform my duties as Director of Operations and then returning home in the evening and seeing three clients, seven days a week, I was diagnosed with Irritable Bowel Syndrome (IBS-D). At one point, I lost 40 pounds. I was quite frightened by the whole experience. The only thing I could stomach day after day was boiled potatoes and carrots as I found it soothing. I started on probiotics and after about six months to a year, I got back to the point where I could comfortably eat other foods. I regained my weight and for the most part, the IBS settled down. I adjusted my diet and ate in moderation.

During this time, my one daughter who was then around 22 years old, chatted to me about how uptight they were around me. They felt they had to look a certain way and act in a certain fashion around me. I was in shock. This would mean I was judgmental like my parents. Who was I to expect this from my children? I spent a long time thinking about this, and to my surprise they were right. I was very concerned that my kids weren't exercising, eating the right foods, watching their financials, and working hard enough, etc. I would like to say I was *just concerned about their health*, but that wasn't true. I was embarrassed about my children possibly becoming overweight and not being perfectly slim like my siblings. I eventually came to the conclusion that this was about me, not about them. My insecurities were revealing themselves through how I looked at my kids. I decided there and then, to stop my judgments with my kids and to just love and accept them. If they did become overweight, they already knew that on their own. They didn't need me to remind them. If they wanted to do something about it, they would. If they didn't, it would be their decision. I was so happy my children had been truthful with me about this. I wanted them to feel comfortable around me. I might never have changed my approach otherwise. I would have died not having a chance to correct this.

> *In fact, I'd suggest that if you're a parent of a teenager or young adult, ask them if there is anything that they would like you to change. You don't have to change anything, but if there is some truth in what they are saying, make adjustments.*

EIGHT

AGE 60: UH-OH! RUN FOR THE HILLS!

L IFE CONTINUED AND then suddenly I turned 60. I fell into a depression. I understood why, but I couldn't shake it. The idea of death started to enter my mind. I used all my techniques I had learned as a therapist to no avail. I called Jane in Holland and had a few sessions with her, but I continued to suffer with this. I could still function and continue my practice, but I couldn't shake the deep dark web of death. I knew I had to expose what was underneath the depression. I decided to try anti-anxiety medicine to calm me down. What I learned firsthand from taking these drugs is that it takes trial and error to find the medication that's the right fit. I also learned how side effects of the medication can affect each person differently. It won't fix everything, but it can help. Many people think it will change who they are and are fearful of it. That just isn't true. If it isn't working for you, you will still have the common sense and patience to find the one that does. It doesn't change who you are—the right one just helps you calm down and make more logical, healthy decisions. Some people are totally against using these drugs, and each to their own. I am all for trying other natural and alternative techniques first, but if nothing is working then I feel that it's better than spending the rest of your life suffering. Mind you, if you prefer to keep making illogical decisions because that is who you are, go for it.

I had some clients who were alcoholics. They would refuse to try any of the anti-anxiety medications because they were frightened of dependency. What they failed to realize, was that they were already dependent on alcohol. If you can move from alcohol to an antidepressant, I would say it was a wiser choice.

Turning 60 made me feel very old. I believed becoming old made me weak, helpless and invisible. It also reminded me that death isn't far around the corner. I started checking for lumps and bumps. Almost any sickness, no matter how common, such as a cold, started making me think it must be cancer. I know I got this from my Dad. I remember when I was a little kid, Dad got a sore throat once and decided it was cancer. He thought that way quite often. I believe the throat cancer scare episode happened at my Bar Mitzvah and you could see the fearful look on his face in the photographs. He ended up being fine.

In the middle of my issues with my illogical fears of bumps and lumps, my wife then got sick. The big C word. She had cervical cancer. I was more terrified than she was. Dianne believed in not getting upset about anything until she knows all the facts. Me, I don't wait for the facts, I go crazy. Well, she finally got the facts and it seemed they had caught it very early. No chemotherapy or radiation was required, although the operation meant a hysterectomy— which took months to heal. She was very brave. The only time she let down her guard was just before we entered the hospital for her operation. The thought of a knife cutting her open took her breath away. She was scared, and to me it felt as if she was almost going to change her mind about going through with the operation. I know surgery is no walk in the park for anybody. We talked for a bit and then we got up and moved forward. She has been cancer-free for over three years.

I worked through my issue with death when I realized that death doesn't make me a weak person. I have no control over it. This is what made me feel weak, the lack of control. I wouldn't let anything or anybody take advantage of me or conquer me. This thought process extrapolated itself to everything, including death. Quite illogical considering that to my knowledge, everyone dies. It is a little unnerving though when you look at a very old movie or a clip from World War 1, and realize that every single person in that clip is dead. Every single person. Regardless, after the above revelation, I became conscious of my illogical thinking. The depression started to fade away and so did the fear of death. The anti-anxiety pill was also helpful.

I have no qualms about taking limited responsibility for some of my successes.

My Dad also died around this time. He was 87 years old. He had prostate cancer and had been diagnosed with Alzheimer's. He used to tell me that he didn't want to die. He talked about having quite an unhappy life. I thought it was so unfortunate that he felt that way. Perhaps he never found his calling. I made a concentrated effort not to follow in my Dad's footsteps.

You can always find happiness in your life if you think about it. Every day there is some happiness (although that's not what I was raised to believe). I was quite sad about my Dad's proclamation about his life.

Dad wasn't really there for me when I was a kid because of his own worries. Later on in life he became my rock. Whenever I was feeling down or fearful, he was there. He had my back. Even though a lot of the stuff he said I had already heard a million times before, it was his tone of concern that comforted me. Now I know my siblings don't necessarily feel the same way about our Dad, but we all have our own perceptions. The way we interacted with our parents would make them react in a certain way towards us. At a young age I realized that if I acted worried and weak in front of my parents they would show me love. They would be able to get close to me. If I was confident and strong, they shied away from me and seemed almost angry at my independence. I believe my siblings were stronger and more confident than I was when we were young – perhaps that was the problem.

As I navigated my way through my early sixties, my wife and I decided to buy a motorhome and go travelling.

We would settle in Yuma for a few months in the winter but I felt unsettled and uncomfortable in the setting. There were lots of activities like pickle ball, hiking, volleyball, golf, baseball, dinners and happy hours, where people would get together and connect. I would join in activities and I would find myself exhausted and anxious every day. This was no way to be semi-retired. I couldn't relax and didn't understand what was going on. It took me time to finally come to terms with this. I believed illogically that if I wasn't part of an activity, I was being shunned. I must be an outcast and therefore unwanted.

These activities were not by invitation. You just showed up if you wanted to. It was so strongly ingrained in my way of thinking – and went back to when I was feeling excluded from the bond my brother's had formed. Also perhaps how I was the black sheep of the family. I finally came to terms with this, I understood how ridiculous it was. Parts of my life became much easier after that, as I didn't feel that I needed to include myself in all the activities to accept and like myself.

I did have one vice aside from loving food. I enjoyed buying things. I wasn't a spendaholic but when I wanted something, it was usually big—and I liked my toys! All-terrain vehicles, motorhomes, cars and desert vehicles – they all gave me a little boost when I wanted to add a spark to my life. Don't get me wrong, I was logical about my decisions, but my wife had to learn how to say "No" to me and mean it. She got pretty good at it. I knew that my toys wouldn't give me the happiness we all want in life, and that they were just a distraction. In fact, it probably made life a little tougher with all the maintenance they required. The novelty of distractions started to wane.

The zaniest purchase I ever made, by far, was buying a dog. I was 64 years old and I picked a breed that didn't know the meaning of the word, "relax". I brought this pup home at the age of 8 weeks. He was a pooping, peeing machine and had to be taken outside every 30 minutes. Basically, I had become a slave to a dog. I thought this was going against everything I was trying to get away from in life. No more restrictions. No more expectations. I was going back and forth on my decision to raise a dog, but my wife fell in love with him. We decided we'd better name this guy, and it took weeks to find the right name. We just couldn't agree. Finally, this crazy dog slid across the floor and slammed into a door. It came to us. "Kramer"! He was a completely black fur ball with a touch of white on two paws and his chest. He had an over bite and was all of ten pounds when he was fully-grown. This guy loves us to death. He doesn't know anything about revenge or judgments. As long as he has a roof over his head, food and water in his bowls and regular belly rubs, he is completely devoted. Unconditional love and forgiveness—what else could anyone want from a relationship? He's an integral part of the family. Talk about pet therapy!

There came a point in my life where I was thinking of retiring from the field of psychotherapy. Not an easy deci-sion. I believed I increased my own self-esteem through helping others. Who would I be without this? But there was another side of me that was struggling with the stress of needing to have all the answers for my clients. People were paying me and they had a right to receive answers. I knew this stress-evoking feeling was not helpful in trying to help clients, and I found myself feeling sad in the mornings. Also, there were expectations of the Psychotherapist College and I was getting tired of other peoples' expectations. Actually, these were my expectations of myself—nobody else's. I didn't like screwing up. I believe that, although this was my calling, things can change physiologically as we get older. I decided to take a chance and discontinue my psychotherapy practice.

I would study to be a "Life Coach". As a Life Coach, the only expectations would be from my clients. But I had expectations of them also. On the other hand, who needs expectations from others in your 60s? I now travel, have a few clients a week which I thoroughly enjoy and I work on my articles and the books I am publishing. I am, for the most part, quite happy with my decision.

Now some people might read my book and think, "this guy with all his issues was a psychotherapist?" I actually found that most of my clients felt very comfortable with me. Why? Because I could easily relate to their issues and they saw that they weren't abnormal. Nothing surprised me. Nothing is *that* bad, and there were ways to find peace if you really wanted to find it.

⤞

But the prodigious thing is, if I hadn't turned around my life in my late 40s, I would be in a pretty worthless place right now. Blaming the world about my lousy luck as a human being. I pulled myself out of the shadows and ended up on top. My struggles and experiences have placed me in a pretty respectable place in my life. I think any therapist who can turn their life around and work through their own demons would probably be in a very decent place to allow them to show empathy to clients and everyone else.

NINE

THE HOLOCAUST: PUTS MY STRUGGLES INTO PERSPECTIVE

I DON'T KNOW WHY this became so relevant to me in my sixties. The only thing I recall is being a child and seeing a black and white film when I was very young. I was about six years old when I was introduced to something that was quite traumatic. A bunch of the local Jewish community gathered at the Dilido Hotel in Orillia. The Holocaust was still fresh in most people's minds, as the end of World War 2 was only 15 years before. I don't know why, but the owner of the hotel had movies of the horrific event. I watched as oven doors were opened to reveal the insides filled with the ashes and bones of Jews. I wasn't sure why we were looking at these black and white films, but I do remember how all-encompassing and devastating it was. From that day forward I had nightmares. The most vivid nightmare focused on Germans burying me alive under a tree. I had so many of these nightmares that I started to believe I had actually been there in another life or consciousness. This was another struggle I endured when I was a child. For a while, the nightmares left me. But as I grew older and reached my fifties and sixties, the nightmares returned and my interest in these human monsters grew. Not sure why my parents and other Jewish families would subject their kids to these horrific scenes, but they did.

I was quite defensive for a large part of my life for many reasons – and I believe one was because of what had happened to my race. They were herded like animals to their destruction and it seemed they did very little to stop it. Never again. We would fight not to allow that to happen to any race again.

When I was around fourteen, I woke up to a sprawling message chalked on our driveway: "The House of the Dirty Jews." We had no idea who did it. I know that as I grew older, anti-Semitism faded into my sub-conscious. I actually thought that people were done with it and had moved on. Later, much later, it seemed to me that anti-Semitism was on the rise again.

But why?

I recently experienced an example of anti-Semitism. I was at a gathering with a number of acquaintances and overheard a woman telling some others that she allows people with RVs to stay overnight on her property. She did it for free. I thought it was very nice of her. She went on to say she'd only had a problem once. She paused to tell the group that she wasn't prejudiced… *but…* there was a couple from Israel who were awful. I shuddered to think that this was going to turn into a story about Jewish people. I started to feel uncomfortable. "They were cheap," she said. I wondered how people could be cheap when the accommodations were free. "It's people like that who give Jews a bad name," she continued.

And there it was.

Right between the eyes.

My wife pointed at me as the woman continued talking. She was trying, politely, to tell the woman that I was Jewish—but the woman was more focused on getting everyone to agree with her way of thinking. When body language didn't work, my wife said, "You don't have to be Jewish to be cheap." The woman looked shocked. Holding my anger back, I said, "Are you saying that Jews should behave themselves because one Jew's imperfection is a reflection of the entire race?" The woman didn't know what to say and the crowd seemed quite unnerved. The conversation came to a quick end. When I returned home, I couldn't shake the conversation. Although the woman seemed kind, her words struck a chord in me.

> *Why is it that people do not realize how their words affect others—no matter how innocent? Are we all guilty of this at one time or another? And where does it end?*

What if—God forbid—a Jewish man was to go crazy and shoot a bunch of people in a church or office?

Would people recognize the person as an individual or would he be referred to by his religion? Yes, there are Jewish people who act dishonourably. But every religion or nationality has dishonourable people. We are human beings. We range from saints to monsters and everything in between. When we think about it logically, we know that one person or a few people, are not a reflection of all. So, I have trouble understanding the consistent hatred of Jews throughout the ages. Even if it were true—that some Jews are cheap and some Jews want world dominance (there is no proof of this), is that a reason to hate? Have we not suffered enough? Over six million Jews were killed in the Holocaust. That accounted for two-thirds of the Jewish population within Europe. Countries around the world refused to take in Jews when the Nazis were ripping Jewish children from their mother's arms and ripping babies from limb to limb. The Nazi army forced people to live and die in inhumane conditions. They tortured and gassed innocent people. They exterminated as many Jews as they could. Very few countries would allow Jews to migrate in the face of this destruction.

And after all that, what have we learned? Anti-Semitism is again on the rise globally.

The terrible truth is that some people think the Jewish community hasn't suffered enough. Some people would like to see us wiped off the face of the earth. Would the hatred stop if we were annihilated? Of course not.

The hatred wouldn't stop because the hate isn't about the object of a person's hate. It's about the person who has the hate.

You can't extinguish the anger by ridding the supposed object of their hate, which in this case were the Jews. Hate runs much deeper than that. It is about the person's own hatred of himself. I am very conscious of a part of me that might choose to dislike others because of the way my people have been treated. But, I know that if I hate, I am no better than the Nazi leaders and their followers.

If you have hate in your soul, find a way to free yourself of this emotion. It will lead to an unhappy life, full of regret. I promise you that.

Everyone is responsible for genocide in the world. We don't get to act innocent and shirk responsibility because it didn't involve us or because we have our own struggles and problems. When you see people being subjected to cruelty in the world, do something. We are all part of the human race. Make your voice heard and take action – use social media, sign petitions and join peaceful demonstrations. But don't turn your back on evil like it isn't your responsibility. I hope so desperately that nobody will ever be allowed to do what Hitler did to the Jews again.

My second thought on the subject:

Human beings can be cruel. I wonder what would have happened if the Nazis had survived and killed every single Jew. Would they have been any happier? Might they have become bored? What would they have done with all that burning hatred? Where would they have directed it next? Wiped out everyone who didn't have German ancestry? All those people who didn't have blond hair and blue eyes?

Maybe the handicapped? What would the world have looked like with only blond-haired, fair-skinned people who spoke German (except for black-haired Hitler)? With hate that deep, would there have been an end?

Let's face it, it was never about the Jews, the colour of the skin, the sexual orientation, the mentally handicapped, the blond hair. It was about a festering anger. It was about a person and his followers refusing to take responsibility for their own weaknesses and fears. It was much easier to blame it on other people. All this destruction, driven by one man simply because he wouldn't or couldn't take responsibility for his own sickness.

Does this not show us how far things can go when we blame others? Does this not teach us what hate leads to? How far could a human being in power actually take that hate?

It happened once and it can happen again. But only if we allow it to.

The scary thing is that Hitler had millions of people follow him. Not only the Nazis, but all those who chose to turn a blind eye. Every country that refused to help Jewish refugees was partly responsible for their deaths.

And now we have caravans of people fleeing South America, many trying to escape poverty, crime, death. They are vulnerable and unsafe. Some people worry that these immigrants will take our jobs. Some feel they will hurt the economy. Some claim that our country will become a cesspool. And politicians… they fear they'll lose votes if they welcome refugees.

So, are we nationalists now? Do we only take care of ourselves? If a man is beating a woman on the street, do we ignore it because we are only taking care of ourselves? Where is our humanity? You might ask, "What about your HATRED of Hitler?" There's no doubt that if he were alive today, he would scare me and my fear could turn into hatred. But, how could I hate someone who was mentally ill? If he'd had only a few others who sided with his deranged thinking, perhaps he would have been seen like the mentally ill man he was. It was the masses of people who followed him, who would have scared me the most. Why? Because a man like Hitler was just one man. The masses who followed him, the people who agreed with his crazy thinking, *they* made a difference. They represented a much more destructive force. They also proved that hatred ran rampant, governing much more than just one man. Now, that is scary.

When life came to be, there was no worldly rule that said that all living beings had to act with kindness. The world we see is the world that is. Most human beings can never be tamed. They cannot be something they are not. And, the human race's ability to hate seems to be growing.

So, you might ask, "What is the answer to all this?"

I once read an article that I can't seem to source anymore, but it described three different ways in which people find happiness. They either live a pleasant life, an engaging life, or a meaningful life. I will explain the way I interpreted it.

Research shows that a pleasant life, which includes a home, a car, a family, etc., does not contribute much to a person's overall happiness. And an engaged life, means knowing your strengths, being good at a task and becoming completely absorbed in it. It's the flow that is satisfying.

But a meaningful life, now that is where you will find the most satisfaction. A meaningful life uses strengths for the greater good. It's something greater than oneself. It's living to help others. It's giving others a purpose. It's living healthily and not hurting others. If we all lived meaningful lives, there would be hope, hope for a better world.

And hope is contagious. There will always be Hitlers in the world. If we all lived with hope, these men would have less impact. And the people desperate for answers would have no one to follow.

This is the will from my Grandfather dated July 12, 1925. It was addressed to my father and his siblings. I don't know if his tune would have changed if he knew what was to follow in Europe. I don't think so, as Jewish suffering has been around for centuries. This was translated from Yiddish.

Dear Children: My last will is

Be honest and just with everyone. Remember you are Jews and study the Yiddish History. You will find that everyone suffers and that all over Jews were not well treated, only because they were Jews. Judaism will never be understood only for one reason and that is because Judaism is built on one strong principle, Justice and Truth. This must always be victorious. Always help build Eretz Yisroel because this is the only thing that can make Jews equal to other people/mankind and bring about a better future one as which they will not suffer as before. Education is the only thing one must pursue in one's youth. Everything will pass or come to an end but education never gets stale.

Regard everyone favourably and don't disgrace anyone. There's no reason for this. Never look down on others. That is disgraceful.

Love others and be good to everyone. This pays very well. Give charity without exception. One must give to everyone who appeals. Give as much as you can. Be friendly to the person, especially to those who have been punished by God so that they have to appeal to others. Never envy anyone because this is not a healthy thing. Besides that other person might envy you. One never knows.

Don't pursue wealth because too much is not always good. Wealth is not always achieved honestly. Also, it is not always satisfying. Live contentedly with your families. That is the best blessing from God. Don't spend beyond your means. Don't look for what you never had. Don't yearn for that which is beyond your reach.

This is my wish for my children, from your Father.

This above will is a good example of what many of us attempt to teach our children and is no different to many other religions and races. Why can't we apply these rules to everyone?

I once asked Dianne a question which could be difficult to answer (and possibly I shouldn't have asked it in the first place). I asked her what she would do if we were married and the Nazis wanted to execute me because I was Jewish and spare her because she wasn't. She said she'd die with me. Now she could just have been trying to make me feel good, but she answered so quickly and matter of factly, that I believed her. She is such a brave, unselfish woman.

TEN

IN SUMMARY...

ON APRIL 30, I retired as a Registered Psychotherapist. This was a difficult decision as I believed it was my calling. I loved helping clients untangle life's issues. It was also a source of great pride for me and gave purpose to my life. One of the reasons I decided not to continue was because of the rules, regulations, requirements, etc. in the province of Ontario. Not that it was necessarily a bad thing, but I preferred the freedom to exercise my own way of applying myself and not be restricted by someone else's guidelines. I have, as everyone else has, lived my life restricted in one way or another. We always will be to some extent, but the less we are, the better. In my sixties, I have earned it and so have many of you.

I have been fortunate to experience each stage of life and there are so many who have been denied this privilege due to early death or illness. Do we ever stop and think how fortunate we are? People in their eighties have told me that they are too young to die. I suggest that if you lived through 80 years of life, you are very fortunate. Try to look at the good side of life and try to accept that death is inevitable. If you have too many regrets or haven't found your passion in life, maybe death will be difficult for you. That is why I tell people to find their passions and to stop the hate. You will have few regrets this way.

Although I spent a considerable amount of time in this book discussing my mother and father's illogical parenting techniques, don't get me wrong. I am sure my kids will have a lot to say about my parenting skills. I know one of my kids think I am a great Dad and the other is a little bit more skeptical about the whole thing. My parents did what they could with what they had. Through this book, my attempt is to show people that most saw my family as being as "normal" as anyone else's. And you know what my thoughts on "normal" are. My purpose in writing this book was to give you some ideas and insights into how to work through your lot in life and to let you know there is nothing to be embarrassed about. Everyone has issues and most judge others, but you have done nothing wrong in just being who you are. We come by our behaviour honestly. The only exception would be that if you know you want to hurt yourself or others, seek professional attention to deal with the issue. There are people out there who can help.

I am now a Certified Life Coach and virtually come and go as I please. I think that is how most of us would like it later in life. If you are in a funk and want some help in moving forward, possibly finding your passion in life, my contact information is:

Email: david@finecoaching.ca

In the Province of Ontario, you must be a Psychiatrist, Psychologist or Psychotherapist to work with clients who have serious mood disorders. Since I am a Life Coach I have given up that healing part of my practice, but I continue to help people untangle life's issues whether it be related to work frustrations, relationships, career or general life issues.

FINDING YOUR TRUTH

I SAW AN OLDER couple in their mid-eighties saunter-
ing along. They stopped to talk to me. Their memories
were not sharp, as they asked the same questions a number of times. When they walked away, I felt full of dread.
I wondered what this was about, this feeling of dread. The
feeling wouldn't go away.

If I wanted to figure this out, I had to look at my
illogical thinking. I had to consider my self-talk. What
was I telling myself? This would take time and concentration. Who wants to do that? I mean, really, I
thought I must be nuts. I had a simple conversation
with an elderly couple, which resulted in being caught

in a web of fear. I could never let anyone know about this. It was hard enough admitting this to myself. It would have been much easier to counteract the feeling or distract myself in some way. Either would have meant I could avoid dealing with it. I could have trained to run a marathon, played a round of golf, spent more time at work, drank a lot, smoked a doobie, ate a few chocolate bars, gone out and spent money or blamed somebody else for my thoughts. While none of these worked well for me, sometimes I found a lazy way of dealing with an issue. The problem with doing this, even just some of the time, was that the dread continued to haunt me. Sometimes, it even grew stronger. So, I still needed to understand what I was going through.

When I met this couple, I thought they weren't living. At their age, they were simply existing. To me, this meant they must be invisible and useless. That frightened me to death. So, of course, my fear wasn't about them at all. It was about me.

I have often said we need purpose to find happiness. I still believe this. Human beings without a purpose might become depressed and as a result turn to drugs or alcohol to escape the feeling. This doesn't mean that having purpose is the answer to happiness, but it might be as close as we can get.

I am now sixty-five years old and I find myself wrestling with my purpose. Why can't I just relax, coast and do whatever I choose? Why do I need to be recognized for my efforts? What does it really matter?

My mindset tells me that being invisible is just existing.

It is, therefore, like death. I also associate "not being recognized" as death. Aha! No wonder I am so frightened of lacking purpose, of growing old.

Now that I realize this, I have come to the conclusion that it's okay to relax. Relaxing does not lead to a dark, lonely place of death. I will continue to remind myself of this when I am overwhelmed, when I feel unimportant, or when I think I am not being seen.

To my way of thinking, finding my truth is much healthier than avoidance. Once the issue is resolved, I do not repeat unhealthy habits.

I hope that some day we can all feel free to express our thoughts with others and not be met with avoidance and ridicule, but instead with compassion and understanding.

How about you?

DAVID FINE

David Michael Fine MA., Registered Psychotherapist (RET)/ Certified Life Coach, has helped thousands of clients navigate multiple issues mostly by reflecting on his own life and personal struggles. His ability to go deep within himself has given him an uncanny ability to assist clients in understanding areas about themselves that has helped them lead more productive, purposeful lives.

His base line therapy was originally centred on "A Course in Miracles" (spiritual transformation). He branched out from there using such techniques as CBT. This was useful in redirecting your negative or limited beliefs.

He has recently retired as a Registered Psychotherapist after 15 years and he now spends his time as a Certified Life Coach helping people find direction in their lives.

He is the author of two books "*Understanding Clarity*" and "*A Book About Nobody*". If you would like to be included in his mailing list full of life inspiring articles email him at david@finecoaching.ca

His website is www. Finecoaching.ca

MAKE SURE YOU CHECK OUT
UNDERSTANDING CLARITY

UNDERSTANDING CLARITY

AN INSIGHT INTO SELF AWARENESS

DAVID M FINE

REGISTERED PSYCHOTHERAPIST AND CERTIFIED LIFE COACH